THE HAMMER AND THE FIRE

THE HAMMER AND THE FIRE

HENRY MARSH

2011

For Alice and Charlotte

Maclean Dubois

Also by Henry Marsh

A *First Sighting*, ISBN 0 9514470 1 7
first published in Great Britain in 2005
by Maclean Dubois,
Hillend House, Hillend, Edinburgh EH10 7DX

A *Turbulent Wake*, ISBN 978 0 9514470 4 8
first published in Great Britain in 2007
by Maclean Dubois.

A *Trail of Dreaming*, ISBN 13 978 0 9561141 0 5
in collaboration with the artist, Kym Needle,
published 2009
by the Open Eye Gallery,
34 Abercromby Place, Edinburgh EH3 6QE.

The Guidman's Daughter, ISBN 978 0951 447062
first published 2009
by Maclean Dubois
distributed by Birlinn.

Printed by CPI Antony Rowe
www.cpibooks.co.uk
Design by Cate Stewart
Distributed by Birlinn Ltd

Acknowledgements

I am grateful to the editors of *Dream Catcher* and *North Words Now* where some of these poems were first published.

I am particularly indebted to Dr Rosalind Marshall for the rich source of detail in her book *John Knox* and for her other work on the Scottish Reformation. She kindly read the manuscript and offered her advice. *The Swordbearer* by my old friend, the Revd Stewart Lamont, was also very useful.

Peter Gilmour provided wise comments, as always, on the selection of the pieces.

But the publication of the collection would not have been possible without Professor Alexander McCall Smith and his team – Lesley Winton, his P.A., and the book's designer, Cate Stewart. I owe them a great debt of gratitude.

The spectacular cover image of the Rosette Nebula I owe to Dr Nick Wright, University College London and the Centre for Astrophysics Research, University of Hertfordshire. I must also thank Professor Janet Drew who very kindly and speedily facilitated what must have seemed a rather eccentric enquiry.

Handing On

The Hammer and the Fire

Introduction

It is likely that John Knox was born in Haddington, probably in 1514. It was during his childhood that Martin Luther sprang to prominence, his ideas being appropriated to justify attempts at social revolution in Germany. The association of religious reform and revolution was later reflected in events as they unfolded in Scotland. Against this background of growing European turmoil, Knox was ordained priest sometime in the late 1530's. The details of his conversion to Protestantism are not known.

The Martyrdom of George Wishart in St Andrews in 1546 had a profound effect on Knox and may have precipitated a choice: should he follow Wishart's example, or work at a safer distance to further the ends of Protestantism?

Following the murder of Cardinal Beaton, Knox was captured in St Andrews Castle by the French and taken as a galley slave. On his freedom, he made his way to England. For the next six years he moved between England, Dieppe, Geneva and Frankfurt.

Knox was happy in Geneva. He heard Calvin's sermons in the sublime austerity of St Pierre's Cathedral, began to study Hebrew and Greek, worked at translation for what would come to be known as the Geneva Bible, wrote and published. In the settled peace of Geneva he saw how Protestant reformation might be fulfilled. In dialogue with John Calvin, he set the question of whether the people of God had the right to depose idolatrous monarchs.

In Dieppe he had worked on *The First Blast of the Trumpet against the Monstrous Regiment of Women*. It is difficult for us to come to terms with his tirade against 'that monster in nature… a woman clad in the habit of a man'. But Knox's target was Mary I of England, that 'cursed Jezebel' and her persecution of Protestants who were being 'consumed in the fire'. Knox argued that it was a *duty* to depose such female monarchs. He was supported in his extreme position neither by Calvin nor other leading reformers.

His stay in Frankfurt was disastrous, marked by vicious in-fighting with Protestant immigrants from England over the Second Book of Common Prayer. Finally, his expulsion from the city was engineered on the grounds of his regicidal ideas.

On a visit to Scotland in 1555-56 Knox visited influential households, taking Bible study and conducting the sacrament of the Lord's Supper in private. He was arguing that no compromise was possible with the Church of Rome. A decisive break was necessary. It was on such a mission that he visited John Erskine at the House of Dun near Montrose, in Angus. The momentum for change was gathering. It would become unstoppable.

He finally returned to Scotland in 1559 where, on the day after a sermon at St John's Kirk in Perth on 11th May, in effect, revolution broke out across the Central Lowlands. Knox had preached on idolatry, attacking the Roman Catholic Mass on the grounds that transubstantiation had no scriptural authority. Knox's notion of idolatry would be defined in The First Book of Discipline: 'By idolatry, we understand the Mass, invocation of saints, adoration of images, and the keeping and retaining of the same; and, finally, all honouring of God not contained in his holy word.'

The next day, a priest celebrating mass chastised a boy for throwing a stone at the tabernacle – the ornate receptacle for the Eucharistic elements – thereby triggering riots and the sacking of religious institutions.

In the following year the Scots Parliament and General Assembly confirmed the Reformation by the adoption of The 1560 Scots Confession. In 1561, Mary, Queen of Scots returned from France but refused to give her royal approval. It was not finally endorsed by the Scots Parliament until December 1567, a few months after Mary's abdication. Knox may well have written the first draft. However, the final version was the work of several reformers and its tone had been moderated. This doctrinal manifesto is surprisingly accessible – it also has an austere beauty.

In 1561 the First Book of Discipline was ratified. Knox and his colleagues had based it on the *Ordinances* for Calvin's church in Geneva. It was a far-sighted document setting out, amongst other things, a vision of education for children – both boys and girls – and provision for universities. Education was not seen as an end in itself, for its aim was to extend the reforming ideology indefinitely into the future – a theocratic vision. But given the times, what else could have been expected? It also argued for provision for the poor. But it shared the fate of most visionary reforms, wanting the resources for speedy and extended implementation.

The Reformation in Scotland was intricately bound up in the dynastic ambitions of France and England. The young Scots Queen had been sent to France in July 1548, some months after the Battle of Pinkie Cleugh and the French King, Henry II had seen the opportunity to extend an empire into Scotland through the marriage of his son to the young Queen.

On the other hand, Henry VIII, had looked to the Treaties of Greenwich to grasp Scotland through the marriage of his son, Edward, to Mary. After the Scots rescinded the treaties, Henry VIII visited a reign of terror on southern Scotland which was furthered, on his death, by the Duke of Somerset – Protector of England during the minority of Prince Edward. The phases of this invasion, the 'Rough Wooing', lasted seven years, between 1544 and 1551.

Whereas, Scottish Roman Catholics looked to France and the Auld Alliance for support, the reformers would look to Protestant England and the Auld Enemy.

After the slaughter of the Scots at the Battle of Pinkie in 1547, the climax of Somerset's campaign, one can only wonder at the social and psychological costs incurred only thirteen years later by the profound shift in alliance, from France to England.

The Queen had returned to take up power in August 1561 and Knox was appalled when she attended Mass at Holyrood. She was an energetic, well-educated, attractive young woman – already a widow, but still in her teens. Subsequently, from the pulpit at St Giles, he inveighed against her idolatry. There followed a series of dialogues where the Queen demanded that Knox give an account of himself. He became convinced that she intended to re-introduce French troops into Scotland to crush the Reformation.

Following the murder of Darnley and her marriage to Bothwell in 1567 – disastrous, both in personal and political terms – Knox conducted what can only be described as a vicious propaganda campaign against her, echoes of which can still be heard in popular myth. But the very shrillness of the voice was, perhaps, evidence of the decline in his influence which had already begun by 1563. He was no politician and as he had said of himself in 1559, 'I am judged amongst ourselves as too extreme.'

There was to be no rest for the reformers. Mary's reign fell into turmoil and she was forced to abdicate in July 1567. There followed bitter and divisive conflict over the monarchy. And Knox could never find peace while she lived. Mary spent her remaining years in exile and house arrest in England until Queen Elizabeth ordered her execution in 1587. She had outlived Knox by 15 years.

The author of *The First Blast* was, perhaps surprisingly, solicitous and compassionate in the correspondence he conducted with women, particularly concerning their spiritual lives. He developed such a relationship with Elizabeth Bowes, wife of Richard Bowes, the captain of Norham Castle near Berwick-upon-Tweed. She became his confidante and a platonic if, perhaps, ambiguous relationship was established between them – he married her daughter Marjorie, a girl in her teens and 20 years younger. But that age difference was unremarkable for the time. They married, probably in 1555. By all accounts Knox was a loving husband and father – they had two sons. Marjorie died five years later, in 1560 and Elizabeth moved to Edinburgh to help raise the young children.

Knox married again four years later. This time the discrepancy in ages did cause something of a scandal, providing scurrilous propaganda for his enemies – Margaret Stewart was 17 and Knox 54. Their marriage also provoked the wrath of Queen Mary. As Margaret was her relative, the Queen's permission ought to have been sought. It is difficult to imagine that Mary would have been delighted by the prospect of welcoming Knox into the family circle. Margaret worked as her husband's secretary and nursed him in his decline. They had two daughters.

In 1571 Knox suffered a stroke and withdrew to Fife. He later returned to Edinburgh and St Giles and died in his home at the Netherbow in 1572. His great achievement had been to lead Scotland to its Reformation and his greatest moments were, perhaps, in the adoption of the Scots Confession and the First Book of Discipline.

At the High Kirk, St Giles'

In the pulpit... I am not master of myself.

This stone house seems built from November,
a spare shell scarred by traces
of lost purposes, where the Word rose,
deflected into resonance by a stone roof.

In winter light, Victorian windows
barely cast their Gothic spell,
though Japanese tourists vaguely smile.
A girl poses for her 'been here' photograph.
They pass without looking a copy
of the National Covenant. I feel a sudden
agitation – some signed in blood, they say.
I wonder where I would have stood.
Probably amongst them. But wincing.

Thou shalt make thee no graven image –
and by the entrance, cast in metal,
the black Knox, that victim of a voice,
his rhetoric a self-seduction where the map
of his going would spread before him
even as he preached – the narrow way
to the Promised Land. It carried him
into a world of signs glittering in their lucidity,
while doubts gnawed only
in the licence of the dark. Mobs roared,
fired by his brilliant fictions, their souls,
like flies, struggling in his God's web.

You wonder where they stowed the whores –
God's image chained in hypocrisy;
and the bloody Maiden's willing arms –
so handy for the Mercat Cross.
In the tourist shop, a postcard shows
light streaming through the east windows.
A dawning that reminds us of the life of Christ.

George Wishart

By St Andrews Castle, 1st March, 1546

Thy foot he'll not let slide –
a psalm wavering from the pit.
That rehearsal for oblivion.
Raised, he staggers, squinting
through the light. Sleepless,
had he caught the dawn's glimmer,
counted the measuring waves?

This unbelievable day.
A sudden scraich of gulls,
fulmars planing on updrafts
along the rocks, wash and roar
of a wintry sea. And dove-down
by the castle wall settled
like a snow flurry. Life expended.

He fought with his eyes
glittered by an east wind.
And the rough rope bit.
Did Beaton smile, his face
stiff in the cold, to see
the Wishart puppet dangling?
Was flame his consummation?

And a choice, Master Knox,
for you? Did you find yourself
in the darkness of Gethsemane?

In the French Galleys

1547-49

Not a time for subtlety.
Icy calms – clamped hands.
Scourged, in chains, hour
on hour at an oar's end.
Interminable, racking days.
Fed by a breath of memories –
till martyrs' embers flame,
a winter beacon. They'd hear
their God speak through him,
set loose their frozen souls.

They lay off Broughty Castle
that rose through summer haar
like something in his fevered dream
he fought to reach. Then out
across the bar, in a west wind,
the veil lifts on Saint Andrews'
towers and the words of Daniel –
My God hath sent his angel,
and hath shut the lions' mouths,
and they have not hurt me….

He reads their bodies' exile,
shows them shimmering Canaan –
their bonds, no more
than filthy spider's webs
he'd sweep away. They breathe
the astringent air of faith,
God's icy, burning Spring.
So Daniel was taken up
out of the den…because
he had trusted in his God.

Berwick

Spring, 1549

Even the rats were dying in Haddington –
and the sick thrown out of the garrison.
We died at the roadside, rotted in ditches,
a black stench by the golden kingcups.
Putte man, woman and child to fyre
and sworde, they'd said. And now we straggled
back through our own infernal making.
We'd watch their grey-faced, bow-legged
children shift through the trees, so many
vermin. They'd strip the crusted rags
from corpses. Up there, Spring brings
famine. So the sight of Berwick seemed
a blessing. Till we entered Hell's citadel.

Houses, nailed tight shut, rocked
in lamentation. Unburied dead seeped
along gutters. The starving murdered
for a clipped groat. Then a crowd in the street.
He looked nothing from behind – small,
black-cloaked. Until you saw the eyes.
Even the strong were abashed. What is
that power? He set God's law ringing
through our heads. Up in the castle,
he commanded our Commander. And by
Christ's blood, set us, so many children,
in right heart. Still we died – but
even our darkest had touched on dignity.

By the House of Dun

Preaching… privately in quiet houses.
Winter, 1555

As you ride by an axe is biting,
grey wood-flakes flying
from the root of a stag-horned oak.
That cold clarity of purpose –
laying waste where you would build.
And all for the meaning of a moment –
This do in remembrance of me.

Did you ever reach from that abstract
labyrinth into the sun? Perhaps
you worried that wind-scurries
along a river, the brush of alder
and willow might be interpreted as
dancing. Was idolatrous wheat
bowing under the golden god?

Did you soar with a blackbird's song?
Or wince at the stab of its blade?
For its prey glistens like the strings
of a drawn martyr. Or like the mole,
prefer an imagined darkness
as you worked along God's purpose
towards a far promise of light?

Oh, you might have been
a son of the morning, were it not
for your justified heart. Driven
by the time's plague – war of heresies –
could the moment of Communion,
presence of the living God,
not lead by stiller waters?

Were you blind to ambiguities?
Or stowed them in the cupboards
of your dreaming? What passed
in that sudden effrontery of the flesh
with Mother Bowes? Deflected
into words and delicate exchanges
impulse could lie in civilities.

From your pulpit at God's centre
I can hear you unfold the awful
sanctions of your vision, watch
that self, armed in righteousness,
swathe idolaters down –
and nowhere more exposed
in disclosure of our animal truth.

From this bridge did you watch
geese fall in thousands
through amber frost haze?
Hear the South Esk, rain-replete,
fold and coil in muttering twilight?
Fear the emerging stars
were deaf to your small voice?

St John's Kirk, Perth

He managed men's souls as he wished.
11th May, 1559

So it is written, *Thou shalt have no*
other gods in my sight. Look round you
brethren and despair, look round
at this profanity, how the pure light of Christ
is stained, how painted idols adorn
the Lord's House. And He sees all,
sees how you kiss the stone feet,
lay your offerings at painted shrines.
He knows your hearts. How odious
are these abominations in God's presence.
Thus are we taught by the apostle,
Abstain from the filthiness of images.

Do you hear that voice from the wilderness:
O generation of vipers, who hath taught you
to fly from the wrath to come?
Do you think to buy your way to salvation?
These baubles, this gilded tabernacle –
would you make of God a usurer? *Now also*
is the axe laid unto the root of the trees
which bringeth not forth good fruit.
Can you see your children, your little
children walking into that wrath, wailing
and gnashing their teeth? *Our fathers sinned,*
and are not, and we have borne their iniquities.

It is not by Christ's body in the bread
that we are saved but by taking Him
into our hearts. In faith alone can we hope,
by faith alone are we justified. Do you dream
you are saved, make idols of your fancy
like Satan's bitches bent on prophecy?
Trust only in His mercy and grace,
take up the armour of righteousness,
weep at your depravity, yea, weep
sons and daughters of Christ. *But that
which is fallen into decay will I build again.*
By true repentance find the water of life.

The Reformation of Lindores Abbey

Is not my word like as fire? saith the Lord;
and like a hammer that breaketh the rock in pieces?
Summer, 1559

'We shove open the doors.
A moment of stillness. A priest,
face grey as a weathered stick,
stands at the altar. He raises
the chalice towards us. Silence.
Altar candles flicker.'

The river's power is constrained –
pent in a slack tide.

'Then someone outside starts
on a psalm. And Bessie Nichol,
her wi' the arms like hams, runs
forward, grabs the altar cloth –
"I'll tak this fur the washin,"
sets their falderals tumbling.'

Along its reaches, sky is translated
into the subtle language of water.

'Then we get amongst it.
Master Knox arrives
all in a lather and some gentles
from St Andrews. "Brethren…"
he shouts. But even as he speaks
worthies are smashing the windows.'

Less than substance, the distant
Sidlaws are a blue dreaming

And Mary, Mother of God –
a people's heart's-ease –
the loved liturgies, holy books
plainsong woven into the soul's
fibres, altars, paintings –
another fiery martyrdom.

The ebb is coiling and winding,
drawing a westerly breeze in its wake.

Grey friars wept in their sarks,
their habits smouldering, nostrils
bitter at acrid desecration.
They watched as ash fell
like black snow trickling
through their fruiting orchards.

An island of sunlit reeds
bristles under the eye of a hawk.

They remembered the eyes – glittering,
glass-glazed, that no sight
could deflect. Guilt, it seemed,
had blazed into indignation. Lost,
they were, to a single soul
burning in an eternal moment.

After *the hammer and the fire,*
houseless swifts are screaming.

Remembering the Field of Pinkie

April 1560

Earth to greedy earth –
the English heretics' swathe
of slaughter. The Esk ran red.

As they stripped the corpses,
they found a white banner
by papist kirkmen – a woman

kneeling before a crucifix:
*Do not forget your afflicted
spouse.* Their church scourged.

As flowers prosper through
the carnage – the little Queen
to France. That Auld Alliance.

Grieve till the wind changes –
and a bitter Spring. Amity
with England. The price.

With sair hairts they fight
their indignation, their weight
of purpose poised at the brink.

She'll bring the lost summer
in her eyes. Though her feet
will falter as the earth shifts.

Loss

Edinburgh, December 1560

That darkness wrapped about him.
But the cold's edge, a purity.
Though the melt in that touch
of December sun – the fire in frost –
fulfils a spirit's craving.
He reaches for a spark.
                    And remembers
Mary – her haze of candles –
the Mother-in-blue. Not
that summer azure of the zenith
but milky, mid-sky blue.
And his mother gone – that tenderness
of women.
                Did he bring unease
to the Table, aware, as a child,
he'd made a deity from loss?
Reading the faces, he knew
their seduction – the broken, come
to worship their despair. He saw
that power betrayed by power –
the subtly crafted rituals, the gilded
oratories.
              And so he brought them
winter, the whirlwind's scourge –
in preparation for the moment:

Eat…
        Drink…
                  And a flooding
understanding
                     that words
                            can hardly
touch: love –

           unconditional,
bound
    to sacrifice.

            Then
nothing remains
        but
          faith.

That scorching clarity.

           And Marjorie
dead – *She whom God hath offered*
unto me and commanded me
to love.… She'd blessed her bairns
that they should be *true worshippers*
of God.
      He holds that truth
for whatever warmth. And walks
with darkness wrapped about him.

Of the Monstrous Regiment

Were you fed by ravens
Master Knox? At the least,
your zealous brethren
obliged with a wilderness
where you could approve
crows nodding
amongst shards and ashes.

Jezebel – how convenient,
the heft of the old stories:
a stolen vineyard,
Naboth stoned,
and Yahweh harrying
your captive souls
half demented.

How neat, to cast
our mischievous Marys
in one image –
a painted whore.
Did you ever catch
in a mirror your own
soul's darker strands?

Thou shalt die the death –
even Calvin winced
at regicide. Were not all
equal in the sight of God?
But who dares walk
that perilous ridge
between iniquities?

De Revolutionibus Orbium Coelestium

Kinross, 1562

A hawk lifts from the Queen's wrist.

'What have I to do with Jezebel?
You abuse the here and now
by the names of the past. It brings you
power, Master Knox. You exult in it.'

'I hear the Word in the instant, Madame,
God's prophetic voice. It speaks
for all time.'

                  'Round and round
you go sir, like a thrawn rat
in a wheel. Your knowledge
is a suffocation, a bewitchment.
It blinds you to the moment.'

'Oh, I see the moment, Madame.
Let me whisper in your ear.
I've seen it in the Canongate in rags
under the snow. A widow and her infant,
their bodies clamped in icy rigor.
No smiling Madonna. Their hands
and faces marbled blue. This
is your realm, Madame, while,
in your pride, you dance your moment.
What has an honest man to do with
fripperies, your masses and masques
where extravagance flows like water?'

'But even you, sir, live in sufficiency.
And I live sufficient to my dignity.
There's a new learning, new
visions. We touch on the Divine
in art and music. Our world changes.
Indeed, Master Knox, it was a Lutheran
had published a book by Copernicus
on the revolutions of the orbs.'

'Nicholaus Copernicus my erse.
Show me, in Scripture, Madame,
where his whimsies can be found.
Our reformation reaches for the Word,
a Bible in our common tongue and schools
to teach our children how to read it.'

An afternoon sun. Their words leap
in frantic gestures along a wall.
Their fiery eyes are locked, blind
to the discourse of their shadows.
A father and his wayward daughter.

'But to where I began – papist priests,
must be punished. Your subjects
are bound in duty to obey you madame,
and you are bound to uphold the law.
If you deny your duty to them,
how can you expect obedience?'

'Master Knox, I shall summon all
offenders and minister justice.'

In Thrall

This wrestling with a wraith.
I suspect, old fellow,
you're cast in my own shadows,
lurking in the struggle to break
from that cold enchantment –
a haunted son of the father.

Sisyphus

1567

The papist whore deposed,
you preached over the head
of an infant king. And now
you have it – a National Church,
the Scot's Confession ratified.

At the summit, did you hear
the mountains singing praises
to the Lord? Or watch clouds
boil beneath your feet? Do you know
the stone will never rest?

And happy you could never be
while the Queen lived – that demon
cast in the Grand Guignol
of your imagining, the woman
you were blind to see.

While the drama of your soul
unrolled, what touched you
through the flickering frames?
Your loving bed-mates, children
and a few fraught women?

One must imagine Sisyphus
happy – you'd never know
our baffled search for meaning.
And all responsibility resigned
to Sinai's crushing tablet.

Bunty Wallace

A windowless hoosie o' glaur
an' turf – wi clorty wains
shewn intae hodden claes,
draggled in rain, airms
reid wi the itch. They bide
wi their granny – dropsical,
drunk as a fiddler's bitch.
Her son gaed fur a sodger.
She doesny ken whit fur,
cares less. They say the Frenchies
gutted him. Nettles an' dockens
in her kailyard. Ca's the bairns
fur their barley cake. They catch
grey doos wi an auld creel
and a bitty string and sell them
for a farthing. A puckle
hens scratch at the midden.
An' oo'r them stands a cock,
a sonsie birkie, wha skraichs
in a' the pride o' roosters.
Priest or meenister – wha
gies a tinker's curse?

Edinburgh

August, 1572

He'd watch them from his windows –
folk below at the luckenbooths.
Youth and age – a rhythm of tides.
Then up the brae that might
have been a mountain, he trauchles, stick
knocking at the cobbles, knowing
that soon the earth would open
and let him in. 'Fine day,
Maister Knox.' He stops, hunched,
like a wet crow on a chimney.
But the voice has passed him by.

Returned to the wilderness –
that barren freedom. He could see
storms crack and rumble
along the skyline. That flickering
play of lightning. But the words
now hard to reach. Grey,
skeletal fingers grip
at the pulpit. Yet the fire kindles.
A doubtful flame. That his days
are ending in peace and honour
is exile for a turbulent spirit.

Gethsemane

By the Netherbow, 24th November, 1572

As you lie this night it seems
the reek of Wishart's burning
is clinging in your throat. Spitting
can't shift it. And now a fevered
resolution into dreaming – a spring
garden, and the spurned serpent
coiled in golden dapple
under a laden apple tree.

And the sun falls, rolling
into the dusk. *Watch with me,*
watch with me, it mouths
at the brink. It seems you stand
outside a gate. Torchlight
throws gesturing shadows
at your feet. They rise, and run
melding into utter darkness.

In sudden, groping blindness
you cry, *I've never known*
the sun. And wake shouting
in denial as the cock crows.
And there is Wishart, the rope
at his neck, his body
cindering against a fiery sky.
He asks the only question –

Have we loved one another?

January 2009

There is but one way to the knowledge
of nature's works; the way of observation
and experiment. Thomas Reid

Snow is blue under the moon.
Shadows search, bold
across frost scorch. Talons
of trees have snatched a victim –
tracks stop by bright blood.

Gutting a rabbit – the hand
grips viscera, pulls
through that cold cavity. What,
Master Knox, can we twist
from your winter landscape?

Authority – grown more subtle?
Flocks, lost in their Bibles?
And Reid, Davy Hume –
the voyagers – set sail
from your Promised Land?

For the thundering word risked
spirit for faith – a yae or nay –
bred righteous indignation
from constraint and bitter charity.
All mirrines is worne away.

And yet, old patriarch,
stinking wounds need surgeons.
Sublime in your assurance, ruthless,
you led that perilous surgery
on the wayward, intricate heart.

Homecoming

St Giles' Cathedral

You set me in a strange land,
Master Knox. Phantasmagoric,
a hall of mirrors, with fleeting
faces the same and not
the same. A traveller returning –
and what do I carry? You bring me here
again – to light, the more
light in its stained passage;
to sound, the more sound
in song. But no distraction –
transfiguration.
          A quiet voice
points to pervasive goodness.
Challenges our indulgent delusion –
the hegemony of wickedness. The liturgy
exalts the hope we nurture
out of suffering, confronts mortality,
the frailty of love. Longing
weaves its rainbow covenant
from our obliteration.
            For time
chimes. And chimes. And in an hour
the earth's inexorable circuit
carries us into light falling
from a south window. It touches,
while we sing, the pair of us.
And something whispers from beyond
my childhood's plaintive seduction –
no leap, for me, no
faith – but joy, a sort of preparation.
Perhaps this beauty – its time
and place – is all that remains
for most of us. A passing
moment. That might be enough.

Origins

Origins

Today your Icelandic blue eye
is sickly grey-green. The socket
bruised, red and ochre. We climb
down the crater, decide to swim,
welcome the warmth. Though sulphurous
mud oozes between the toes.
Viti – they say this is the mouth of Hell.
At Krafla we walk hot crust,
a tortuous honeycomb, razor-edged.

Like infernal porridge pots, fumaroles
slurp and burp. By a row of houses,
beyond the washing, gouts of steam
writhe in the chilling air. Heads
bobbing like seals, we dine in a pool,
slowly wrinkling white, postponing
the moment – a dash across snow.
By the Lake of the Midge, drink soup
with surfing blackflies in our bowls.

Sea-born volcanoes, fjords
and dragon chasms – a primal landscape,
God-forsaken, though here and there,
black cinders flower in tufts
of thrift battered under ice-cap winds.
And by its turbid, snow-melt rivers,
Arctic willow herb, dwarfed, yet in a purple
flaunting. Thor's ravens voice
the spirit of place in sooty croaks.

You catch how worlds evolve
from stardust, life from the crucible.

Oasis

I offer a heavenly philosophy in place
of the heavenly theology.... Johannes Kepler

We return from Askja across a desert,
lurch and judder through lava fields,
brown plains of ash and gothic boulders.
Astronauts trained here. Late in the evening
we arrive at an oasis – with flowers and birds
and crouching willows. A great moon
hangs over the Lindaà. Its shines,
that other desert, reflects in the river.

You can just see Kepler's Crater
where a Jovian thunderbolt slammed
into the dust. Johannes saw the cosmos
as the Book of God, its revelations
disclosed to reason, the score of its harmonies
written in numbers. John Knox
derived a Witchcraft Act from Scripture –
under the pane of deid... to be execute.

Mother Kepler will be tried for witchcraft.

Kepler's Supernova

October 17th, 1604

Ophiuchus, the Serpent Bearer –
they say he was Asclepius, a healer
who could raise the dead. So Zeus
killed him. These jealous gods.
But then he thought him worthy
of memorial and drew him in a constellation.

Kepler studied his wounded foot
inflamed by an angry star.
A thermonuclear abscess – the physician
afflicted. Saw stellar
death throes, flesh roasting
into vapour, flinging into the void.

A blaze that burns to soot
and sand, forges new elements –
that nudge into a ball. And the dance
begins again. And our rain
of stardust nurtures – our wheat
grows tall. A moment's resurrection.

Cognition of Torture

September 28th, 1621

Katharina Kepler, guilty of witchcraft –
the evidence too thin for a burning.
After fourteen months, a final throe.
She's taken to the place of torture. Stained
walls and floor, stench of the slaughterhouse –
blood and urine. One by one
they bring their toys, like boys with a wounded
frog or stranded jellyfish. Flesh
cringes from the breath of spitting irons.

    She won't confess.

They flourish the prickers – bee-sting
hooks that fish out gobbets of flesh.

    She won't confess.

And the rack and wheel to un-joint bones.

    She won't confess.

And the agony of burning – rehearsal for Hell.

    She won't confess.

Aged seventy four, the stubborn hag.
She rode a calf to death, made cows
unruly. Her touch brought agony.

They exhaust their games. A final harangue.

    She won't confess.

Legless as a drunk, she's slumped in chains,
flesh raw where the shackles bite.

They drag her to the light of day. Release.

Held in that underworld, her sunken eyes
are hard to reach. Then she feels the touch
of an autumn sun. Sparrows are chirping,
a cart passing – our improbable life.

The Mystery of Tides

Like magnetism, he thought,
the influence of sun and planet.
It solved the mystery of tides.
And if it governed the system –
why not ourselves? A reluctant
astrologer. No power in the pattern –
the accidental scatterings of stars –
no power in events. More,
perhaps, like bright or gloomy
days insinuating influence
on our souls. Yet, how profound
that planetary pull – evolving
wings of birds and butterflies,
the buoyancy of fish and whales,
the limbs and spread of trees –
those soaring gantries proffering
leaves. Our bone-braced gait.

Harmony of the World

1619

Opposite the gate
of our country churchyard,
a roe buck, limbs
poised in the grace
of that effortless leap,
antlers gloved
in a May velvet.

But the eyes glazed –
blue bloom
of a ripe sloe –
jaw dropped
in the gape of a gasp,
hide torn
from the ribs – pink-
stained shock-white.
And viscera? Gone
to the prowling fox
and early buzzards.

Recall the lion tearing
at the pulsing innards
of the twitching wildebeest.

The ear of the mind,
he thought, is attuned
to God's harmony –
but the notes of the Earth
sing in lamentation.

And the churchyard gate,
that promise of entry,
now unreachable.

Rainbows

Our duty… will appear to us by the light
of Nature. Isaac Newton, *Optics*

Seven months they tossed
and groaned. Then a grinding
lurch and the boat stranded
on a mountain top. The bloated,
stiff-legged carcasses long
sunk – so the raven found
no cause for hope, returned
bedraggled. Though fish prospered,
nibbling shrimp multiplied
and crabs stalked, hopeful,
through drifts of shining bones.
So half the world was glad.

None seemed moved to task
their fearful God. No
fists shook from the deck.
Then a dove returned with summer
in its grasp. Tearful in their joy
they stowed the tarpaulin roof,
let in the sun. Roars and bellows
from the hold – a skylark sang.
And slowly, only slowly,
as if waking from a dream,
they fumbled to their questions.
He soothed them with a rainbow.

Newton's professorial God
was strangely like himself – thought
in equations. Hardly genocidal.
The ultimate Aesthetician would make
no mistakes – for incoherence
is dissolution, nothingness. So time
would flow across the master plan
explaining every nook and cranny,
the dazzling symmetries. Through a hole
in a shutter, he'd catch a sunbeam,
split the light, explore the rainbow –
the *wonderful composition of whiteness.*

The Watch

Black-and-white, they say –
the old photographs. Or infinite
shades of grey? Pin-striped,
old-man-of-the-sea, grandpa.

He'd mended my yacht – stepped
a mast, stitched a sail.
Too well. Next day, away
it bobbed. Into the North Sea.

Shades of grey. But ticking
in his fob, his gold watch –
that oiled and wheeled universe
hidden behind the face of time.

Swung from its chain – like the clock's
grave pulse – it became
a pendulum talisman to soothe
a fretful child's upset.

At Hogmanay, that marks our turning
into the sun, their house would throng.
Sleepless, in a spare room,
I'd toss on pitches of laughter.

Lost in a Highland reel,
my aunts would weave and wheel
across the rocking room, creators
of another time and space.

But imagine star dust
at its dance unfolding through
many dimensions. And a God
who might, after all, play dice.

Lux

Behind the house
where all the clocks
have stopped, shadow
is in retreat. Light,
from its seamless passage
fragments in the agitation
between air and water.

A pair of grebes
dance in the dazzle.
Eyes, ghosted
by the hurt, are soothed
in the grass. Pearled
webs echo the encounter
between light and water.

Be careful where
you walk – there are flowers
beneath your feet.

Lumen

Morning arrives
at a rose window.
As light reclaims
this sacred space
jasper and sapphire
bring consecration.

*

The green reflected,
comforting the eye –
but red and blue
within the leaf transfigure
our exhausted air
to flower and seed.

Illumination

The red and the blue –
blood and spirit.
Primal antagonism –
our need for redemption.

How holy words
translate the light,
people our emptiness.
That veiled appropriation.

Blood stirs for the power
born from spirit.
Moth from the chrysalis –
the death-marked *Atropos*.

How far from the carpenter –
warmth of the sun –
this glass and stone,
this cult of suffering.

And yet – by glass
and song and word,
this theatre of the soul
mines beneath the mind.

Creates accommodation –
a fit space
for solemnity – points
to the vines' reversion.

Frees a frozen lock –
till that door closes
and we shift away
with only our thirst.

Light and Water

Slow, deliberate
             bulked dark –
like something
             sacred –
                    through fog
a horse
       led by a girl. Their
substance is
             uncertain.
                    The lane
bends,
       unfolds.
                    Gone. You look
beyond
       the hedge. Did they
                         disperse,
their warp and
             weft some trick
of light and water? You feel their
                              presence
the stronger for their
                    absence.

                              If
there were
             spirits
                    they would know this.

You follow a dead oak's
                    gestures
through thinning grey

to the
hint
of a wash of blue –
elusive.

By nightfall, you find the fog's
edge –
a startling
yawn
into darkness. The stars
are crystal-
sharp with frost. As you
reach
they fall, fall
back
into oblivion.
Something
is stronger in its
absence.

Dancing after Bees

Thinking Path

Darwin at Down House

They're not things that we choose –
the beloved place or face. They
choose us. Beyond Great Pucklands Meadow
the patch-worked greens of June woods
are shifting in a warm wind. In a photograph,
the old man looks haunted, his eyes
shadowed under the brim of a sombre hat.

I look – but like a five-year-old, can
barely read: ash, beech, hornbeam;
ivy stalking through stems of seeding
blue-bells, gathering for a leap
into a likely tree. A thrush threads
the bead of an eye on the hint of a target.

He set his children dancing after bees
to trace their mind-maps; plotted
with FitzRoy-precision their navigation
of Great House Meadow; heard
fledgling Magpies squeal like damaged
rabbits, watched them gape for kicking
nestlings; passed stinging nettles
cradling the youth of delicate butterflies.
God's smile withdrawn, his world
glittered, relentless in its raptor beauty.

An oak groans in the wind as it hoists
laborious boughs through the grip of the planet.
Its roots feed in the litter of decay
that gathers on an ancient sea's skeletal
siftings. And the bedrock tidal – its rhythms
obscure in our imaginable time.
The mind, he wrote, *is stupefied
in thinking over the long... lapse of years.*

The fathomless eyes. He knew how love
wills a momentary, unreasonable
stasis. Were there mornings when
he fought his vision? Nights of vertigo?

Sundew – Loch Druidibeg

Think of orchard pleasures –
fruit red-ripe,
and polished to ignition.
The urge just to touch –
then the resonant crunch
of the first bite.

Think of the ocean
undulations of this moor
and the warm lure
of harbour lights, sweet
with homecoming, as angry
darkness falls.

Think of an aerial
coal-house particle,
drawn down
through wafts of myrtle
to clusters of stalked,
red-cherry eyes.

And the first honey touch
traps the tongue. Legs
tread super-glue,
frantic wings heave,
eye stalks tear.

Already the brain is
dissolving, entrails
martyred to fiery enzymes.
Black husks
are trembling under the wind.

At Loch Cròcabhat

Impatient with June's gloaming
the sun yawns over Aisgerbheinn.
Where the flow of light is collecting
pale ephemerids glitter, as if born
for this moment of interception.
Thinnest stems of budding lobelia
double in pink reflections.
The far shore is set in liquid silver.

Then a breeze. You look up.
A wind flexes. A car is passing
on a distant road. Look back –
the loch has hidden in the familiar.
Though that awakening moment hovers
like an after-image at the edge of the eye.
You remember that the day
is something that you look behind.

Black and White

A cats-paw
        scribbling
between lilies? Then
              you catch
the pattern –
        black-and-silver,
rudderless
        power-boats –
whirligigs. Calm
           soothes.
The lochan opens
on lustrous
        watery enigmas.

Bi-focal beetles –
           how odd
to see both
        sides
of your horizon. Unlike
ourselves who
          blink
between our magpie
worlds
      of black
         and white.

October 1st

Sullen, mizzling – the morning
scowls like guilt beneath a secret,
till sunlight forces a window,
looks in, floods. And a press
of cloud retreats to a gloomy
brooding along the hills.

On a bank of holly, webs,
open as palms, are belayed
to prickles on a sheer face.
Layer on layer they hang
heavy with hoarded rain
globed and bright as quicksilver.

My touch, like an impossibly
galumphing fly, fools
no one. Except a single,
yellow-striped gambler
that picks its way through glitter
stalking a dream of plenty.

But its time will come, its web
thrum, its jaws close
in some blur-winged iridescence
or leggy blob drawn,
like a moth to the flame
burning in each drop.

At the Window

Hair-cracks in the glass?
A daddy longlegs.
What holds it there?
And the window in gentle,
August grief. The tiny
drumstick gyroscopes
that set your flight
and your sea-horse head
are still. What shreds
of impulse lift and
settle you? What world
do you travel? Raised up
from the grass roots,
you've thrown away
your leather jacket
to risk the uncertain
air. What revelation
as you broke from the earth
into the swingeing light?

Such awkward
delicacy – you cling
to the nothing that's there,
baffled by its peevish
invisible obstruction.
Where we would find
a barrier of the mind
to explain exclusion
from that inner room
we never reach.

Marsh Thistle

Cirsium palustre

Bloodshot, purple eyes, bleary
in the wind, are open to the terns'
garrulous inspection. Awkward,
Neanderthal arms droop.
These thistles are no canny Scots,
though they share the instinct
to snap at the wind, recoil and
stab. But Autumn is reaching them,
time's drought. Age, as
always, is at war with the sap.

Old warriors, they yet maintain
some semblance of order,
ranked on this sodden knoll
in the gestures of glory days.
Their forebears saw drekkers
sleek over the voe – dragons
with bones in their teeth. Fagged,
fashed, at the end of their summer
campaign, their final humiliation
is to be ravished by delicate butterflies.

Like to Like

After a night's rain, a rich
September sun – it might be tasted
on the tongue. In a few early-cast
leaves a peacock butterfly,
its wings canted – a door
ajar, as if held, paused,
by a stubborn life-glint
before closure. It stirs,
frail in the warmth of my hand.

I carry it to the greenhouse, place it
in a tibouchina flower – a purple,
silken flounce, a remnant
glory from a Brazilian carnival.
Like to like. And if no
revival, at least a death
touching something beautiful.

In the shadow between the wings,
in a red darkness, an eyespot
glimmers like a planetary shining
crossed by a constellation of five
remote blue stars.

This morning, in a litter of petals,
there's a dried winter leaf.
Frozen in that final fold.

Glen Esk

Red sandstone – the river
has ground across the grain,
its sills breached and battered
by stone-clubbing bree.
In black pots and holes
eddies twist and simmer.

Stacked up the gorge, tiered
beeches shift on the breeze
in a slow, ocean swell.
Mayflies dip and swirl
over honey-gold reaches
in the sunlight of their single day.

Swallows cut through thousands.
Spinners, wings prone,
glide on green reflections towards
cascades. At the tails
of pools, glutted trout
dimple in lazy slurps.

And the future drifts like dust
through shafts of wrinkling light,
catches in gravel, nudges
under weeded stones, begins
that crawling, bug-eyed infancy –
all for a moment's dance.

By the Sound of Eriskay

A bundle of
                  angles –
                              an
awkward
          grace – a
Giacometti
                  stood
in a tidal pool.
                  An absence
in grey
          till the neck
                      snakes
back.
      The weapon
                  aimed –
it
   stabs,
          A heron shakes
its head in a bright rain
and
      swallows. You watch
the slow
          slide
                  down
the endless
              throat.

Stonechat

An eye. With wings. The tense
tail flexes. He falls into the grass,
works upwind along a fence.
Collared soot and ember, he darts
and hovers, a diver into depths
of green, gathering pale moths.

His mind patrols the insect
world, computes its subtle
encryptions where a scrap might
suddenly lift and fly,
or he grabs at a blur of air – but
aware of the treacherous sky.

For a claw might strike
from the unaccountable wind.
Though the ghost has folded,
for a moment, on a pole. Noisy,
in its wake, peewits twist
and drop into a restive silence.

Valhalla

For Bill Neill

Locked on a fence post,
Ketil Flatnose, machair
marauder, daylight owl
with a moth manner, fresh
butter-blond but mud
spattered, beak seemingly
battered at the tough wall
of his china egg. He barks.

Slowly, in passing, we lever
his head round the axis
of his indignation. He launches,
dog-fights with a lapwing,
slides down a drift
of evening sunlight, rises
like smoke, skims a wash
of dark pink sedges,
tips down the beams
of his yellow searchlights
at a mesmerised vole.

With lazy flaps he lifts
and drifts in a 'V' for victory
glide. Lost in a daydream
of satiation, he strays
to a butter-cupped meadow –
veers from the invitation
of a million yellow eyes.

Kestrel

A kestrel, hunched on an oak
under a March snow-shower, russet
as the dead leaves by its shoulder.
Behind its head, furtive sunlight
sneaks along the hill. Clamped
in that yellow foot, the tree
is restive. The bird broods –
that dark, stilled eye.
It waits for the sun to nudge
a wider passage, open
a window on a small fear
crouched in the ochre meadow.

It often sits on our wires, lifts
away when we turn the corner.
Drops an occasional scrap
of vole head and once
a bit like a fur thumb
amputated from a mitten.
Tapped by that elegant ferocity
hints of our lives thrum
under its grip – it's well that we
crouch under slate and stone.

Voyager

On a Swallow found in a garage.

You'd see that strip of gold July
under the edge of the metal door,
how sunlight round the edges
fans into ambiguity. Your summer
resolved into desperate, crepuscular
bat flights above spiders
that would nourish were they not
lost to your aerial domain.

And the mind that would steer
its passage along earth's
looping power lines, baffled.
Though almost as light as air,
the slow drag of hunger
conspired with the inexorable planet,
pulled you to a threshold where
wings themselves began to weigh

intolerably, just carried your final
weariness to lodge on the ledge
where you thought to have nested.
Your head is fixed under your breast
in a gesture reaching for comfort.
And that extraordinary voyage
that carried you from primordial time
stopped by a steel wall.

Colonsay

April rides in from the Atlantic.
Hooves of its cavalry slash
the running strand. Shower
banners whip and curl.
Stubborn in their acres of sand,
the sills that root the island
assert their illusion of permanence.

Slate-green waves shatter,
throw their prodigal light
at the sun. A hoodie craw
is not distracted. Blind
to pyrotechnics, he beats
his presbyterian way
through the snorting wind.

It might be the choughs
are playing. Fingered pinions
stretched, they rodeo-ride,
dip and glide in chattering
nonchalance. Scraps of black
silk, they fling into a gully.
The rocks swallow them.

Rain-washed

Did the house shake? Or just
me? That flash – that whip-lash
crack. Then a downpour
dancing on the grave of the day
and the air sweet-smelling.
A thinner rain sets in,
rides on a sudden breeze.

And evening song doused.
A solitary bird drops
out of the grey, all flame and
cinder – like a manifest memory
of the storm. Or has the torn air
let pass a glimpse of life
just cast from the furnace?

It settles, feeds – this improbable
articulation of dust – a goldfinch.
For bird and glistening flowers,
the tiered trees, have tipped
into strangeness – rain-washed,
lightening-scoured, the eye
of the mind has broken free.

Dirt-tosser

I'd expect you to be earthy as a root.
But there you are, you pale-palmed
swimmer – mouldywarp – spruce
as a blackberry. For days it's rained –
are your galleries flooded? Did you think
to take the improbable sun?

With eyes unseeing, pauses
to dig and delve, you're somehow
professorial. I imagine you an expert
on the textures of soils, their implications
for engineering and the unearthing
prey/mole speed ratio.

I'd pick you up. But remember
stories of a toxic bite –
and my fingers like pudgy worms.
I'm worried about traffic – stand
in your way, stamp my foot.
Your nose whiffles. Deflected.

When I return, there's no wee
doormat on the road. And my reward –
a meandering furrow on the lawn.
And two exploratory pits.
Oh well – like most of us,
you're too blind for gratitude.

Trickster

Loki's hunters swept the pool –
he slid between two boulders.
When the net dragged up it held
a rag of weed and lozenges of air.
They weighted it with stones –
a turf cave swallowed him.

Keen eyes discerned the neb,
rebuilt half the head from shadows –
they trudged home for their spears.
His water magic bent the shafts –
tines turned on pebbles. In a cloud
of gold-flecked sand, he bolted.

Loki's wit is belied by the little
eye. His whole body thinks, fed
by the subtleties of flowing water.
Salmon-wise, from cool shade
he studies columns of wrinkling
sunlight whose shifting angles

measure the day. He dreams
of palaces fit for a god.
But the scaly knees of herons
in warming meanders, dippers
sleeked in silver bubbles,
confront him with the shallowing reality –

a quivering consummation over
rough gravel, an exhausted
drift to winter seas where once,
the salmon glowed silver, thrumming
like tuning forks to the spectral
singing of the looming whales.

Loki decides he'll play the god.
He'd rather crackle in the hearth. Too
late – Thor grabs him by the tail.

Belhaven Bay

The Bass Rock's guano-grey
might be vaporous, a silk-sheer
garment lit by the sun, were it not
that the gannets' merciless white
destroys all ambiguity. They lift
the eye to cobalt wind-roads,
cloud-down feathered. Gulls
in a raft, green-billed, are dipping,
dipping through the panes behind
the broken waves – the pulse
of a running tide that soothes
and smoothes the sand planes,
nudges a bubbled scum, a scurf
that wriggles. Ghosts of commas,
black pin-head-eyed, x-rays
of tiny embryos are hectic
in the swirl as if in a fury
of begetting. They stretch in cosmic
millions, these doomed ecstatics,
along the wide miles of a bay.

Mummy

A stranded dolphin in the sand.
The skin has shrunk like a wet coat
along the contours of the spine. Flies
walk through the ragged socket
of an eye into the cavern of the skull.
Do they hear the hiss and roar
of the sea, echoes of the exultant
breenge and lunge at electric
mackerel? The skin has split
on the lower jaw, exposed
the bone heft of a weapon
studded with nails. Mummified
in sand, stone-stilled in the attitude
of speedy passage, it witnesses
the rhythm of tides, the slow
procession of light and dark.
And now, in the dusk, the Atlantic
is pouring from the mouth of a furnace,
a scorching road from the west.
I see Cnoc Hallan in the distance,
that knoll, where for some, the dead
are a harvest, where meaning grows
like grain on the waving machair.

Beach at Smeircleit

Strange, shifting flashes
along the tide-line. We trace
the dazzle to kelp in sea-fresh
tangles – olive, amber – and
where it twists into the light
it glitters. Foam is quivering
in the wind, juddering up
the sand, so many ribbon
galaxies singing back
its passion to the evening sun.

This flooding peace. Then
how do we turn, leave this?
Step slowly, slowly
on our homeward journey?
The day is behind us falling
into the ocean's chill. We follow
our footprints back to tomorrow,
know folk will come
and find a tide, a light –
the moment spilling like water.

Drove Road

Torchlight fingering the path, groping
for some purchase on the familiar – and stags
moaning, roaring. A savage chorus –
as if these ancient hills had found a voice
raised from the phantasmagoria of dreams.

Dreams don't have edges – they brim
the mind. Unlike walking the day
and the thresholds we cross in encounter –
for it's others who make us. The dog
by the fire dreams its pursuits – the twitch
and whimper – and beyond that world
a room, a house, the night. And the lost –
adrift in brimming dog dreams?

A blue-tit at a feeder – its cap
fluoresces, catches the mating-minded.
And flowers lit up like landing strips
for butterflies and bees. And bat computers
flying blind through sonar maps….
Hints from beyond our edges. While here,
frost makes the stags' electric darkness
tingle. And the Hale-Bopp comet hanging
on the north like a celestial gamete.

We stumble our torch-lit way through
all the strangeness of this dispensation.

Echidna by Three Pine Trees Quarry

For Kym Needle

Travellers through another time
wandering their universe of ants.
Flesh or fowl – who could dream
the Echidna? Bits from an ancient
scrap-yard glued along a tongue.

Diggers and delvers: they claw
through termite towns – we cleave
through rock. The wall between us
is within – for lost to ourselves,
who can think Echidna?

Imagine licking the earth,
tongue searching the sear
for glistening acid-drops,
at the tremor of soft foot-falls,
curling behind your palisade.

To find a language to render
their mystery would restore us
to the earth. And the shadows
at their dreaming – can we sing them
back into the dignity of substance?

Handing On

Sun-dust

Flowers in a vase – born
for sterility. Purple, daisy-white –
their dry petals nerveless
in a still room, gold mounds
of their sex unvisited. Their smudge
of beauty is hardly noticed –
fulfils none of our obligations.

Outside, daffodils are barely
tethered in an rough-house wind.
Though celandines squat tight
under sparring shadows. Sun-dust
shakes from willows, a thrush
swings on its mast-head as April
shimmies through pollen and song.

Lindisfarne

A black horse in a small field.
   Its enamel bath is tilted,
collects the cold October light
   pouring from the west on a wind.

It picks its careful way along
   its mind-path – a figure
of 8 tramped to mud, tight
   in a corner of its nettled world.

Head bowed, round and
   round it treads – though
always it stops by the barred gate,
   raises a liquid stare.

The eastern edge is a priory wall.
   You imagine black-cowled monks
intent on their paths of the spirit. Round
   and round, heads bowed,

they pass through their Book of Hours,
   their ritual year. Stone slabs
enclose the bones of Celtic fathers,
   the ecstatic wanderers.

Jupiter

In mid-channel, the 'Jupiter',
smart in black and white, moves
with swan-necked grace to some
assignation in the North Sea.

Two hornets cavort in its wake.
Snowboards with engines, they streak
inshore on the bounce, engraving
their ciphers on leaded glass.

Round the edge of a wall, surging
into the harbour, a dozen swans,
a harried squadron, their necks
stretched over audible bow-waves.

They find composure in a mirror, dip
to greet themselves in confirmation.
It seems they're sketched in charcoal –
then you see they're smeared in oil.

Wheelhouse – Cille Pheadair

Under the plaintive fuss of oystercatchers
the tide is mooching through rotting kelp
humped in sky-burials – for whirling flies.
Stalks stick out like thigh-bones
of great prehistoric birds. Behind a lip
of dunes, the ruins of a Wheel House –
late Bronze Age, they say. And vaguely
disappointing – you'd half hoped to surprise
a ghost. Though the long light slanting
the machair might, at a nudge of the wind,
twist into the lonely shapes whose voices,
at the edge of hearing, are talking on the wind.

Tidy wives, who swept their floors,
have kept their mysteries. A slattern's midden
is more helpful – we re-build lives
from rubbish. And when our house of cards
is blown away, could we learn, again,
to make fire – cosset those frailest
flint-life sparks? Build with numb hands
a refuge from the rain, from ugly neighbours?
Fallen further back, could we hunt and gather?
We'd watch our children grow round-bellied
and as our knowledge frittered into myth,
would we gather simples under a full moon?

Eco Demo

You stand with a placard, smiling,
lost in your conviction. With forty folk
of middle age. I dither. Wander about.
Why can't I join you? I believe
what you believe – with no less passion.

But slogans make me prickle. Denial
of reasonable dialogue? Even soliloquies
talk with themselves. The absurdity
in gesture? Embarrassment at display?
There's something here I can't resolve.

Suddenly you fall into remoteness –
the girl that I married now a woman
in a crowd. That other solidarity.
There's a chilly wind. I touch,
for a moment our primal loneliness.

Policemen pass. The square empties
through city traffic – relentless.
Its roaring brims the city canyons.
It echoes all over the planet.
Hand in hand we walk away.

At the Royal

Broken ribs, a smashed cheekbone –
he'd fallen, the old man in the next bed.
Worked thirty years as a miner,
smoked like a chimney. His lungs seemed
almost solid, his coughs heaving
in their Iron Maiden. I lay wincing,
dragged out of shallow dozes.

He keeps canaries – thirty birds.
Down in endless galleries, the deepest
mine in Scotland, his mind took
flight to summer evenings, pulling
shepherd's purse and chickweed
for his nestlings, wandering country roads
for queen of the meadow.

For a few seconds, they'd said,
it would feel like dying – perhaps
it did. Who knows. And I remembered
Keats in his dream dying into life,
transfiguring that deadly rehearsal,
lifting from the galleries and flying,
light-winged into song.

Walking through the Gorbals, I passed
so many – pubs and betting shops
and dark-lit caves offering
tropical fish. You image cramped rooms,
with wee windows opening on darting
effulgence. Dreams and gleams
of other worlds – how else could we live?

Singularities

Naked singularities – sounds
racy. I sit here reading, re-reading –
loop quantum gravity – resigned
to accept it as reportage, my mind
agape as a child's mouth
open in wonder. Return
to this chair in a hospital ward.

Outside, a crow sits in a recently
planted tree – leafless as yet.
Thin, nursery straight.
Someone has painted the cold
in lead cloud. *The star*
crumples to a pinprick. You feel
the frailty of wonder, how it's drained
by circumstance, shrinks to this grey
that draws everything into its winter.

That monotonous sonar beep
is someone else's heart-beat,
a life poised on the knife's edge –
sleeping pills and a bottle of wine.
She's young. So young. Her man,
unshaven, flushed and drunk,
is slumped in a chair by her bed.
Bound – in love and suffering?

Paulo and Francesca – caught
in that inferno, souls tormented
by memories of lost, happier days.
At what moment did her fingers
loosen, her grip fail,
her spiral begin into that black hole?

Stroke

A cold sky is thinking in clouds.
Grim, heraldic – they're driven
in a clawed scurry. Scourged
apple blossom litters the grass.
What words are reaching for articulation
in this anguish so urgently dumb?

At our last meeting, leaving
the grip of your eyes was a wound
that I salved with the promise
of early return. As I left the ward
I turned my back on linties' nests
in the whins, black capped
goldfinches spearing at thistles,
the twitting flight of greenfinches,
new hawthorn in its green grace.
You taught me how to look.
And with a look we parted.

Inheritance

We'd spent an afternoon howking
tatties. Smoke-cured, his amber
fingers were grained with the earth
he'd worked. Their calloused grip
held aunty's china cup
precious as a finch's nest.

Shadows of a sycamore, heavy
with the croon of pigeons, sat
by him on the garden seat.
Old roses, their scent
caressing as velvet, stirred
with the urgent crawl of bees.

We'd search the evening sky
to find the laverocks. And out
of their song they'd fall,
quivering wings wide – that
rhythmic glissade. Discrete
as dew, they'd settle in the grass.

Child at your hurry – we pause
to watch a sparrow bathing
in the dust. You little know
that three of us are here.
And something to pass on – too
much. And not enough.

At South Lochboisdale

For Dòmhall Aonghais Bhàin

As we cross the croft to your house,
I hear you at my shoulder – your verse
    on the bards' memorial – and look
behind to Loch Boisdale, its intricate,
    shifting azure and turquoise
set within rock and ribs of skerries –
    what you saw from your window.

Blue twine holds the latch.
The door staggers on rusty hinges,
    its planks, like broken teeth,
grate over fallen plaster. The ceiling
    gapes, opens on beams
with their flora of rot perilously bridging
    the murk in the pitch of the thatch.

Your photograph lies warped
on a dresser and a framed letter from a prince.
    Our dismay is for you, but in that void,
for a moment, our own fear flutters
    lost in that dereliction before
the dubious sweetness of the picturesque
    has stripped you from your walls.

No children but your song.
I remember a boy three months
    in the water. Now other eyes
are groping to discern, find marks
    for navigation through the driven rain
to run their keels through surf
    into the peace of homecoming.

And song? Here and there
we catch it, transposed from white
     shell sand – that drizzle
of the dead – and tangle in its stink of decay:
     drills of oats in garlands
of marigolds and peewits tumbling in a wind
     honeyed with the scent of flowers.

Dandelion Clock

Annie Darwin at Down House

Did he ask you the time, Annie?
Three puffs – and dandelion
down adrift, that gentle
fall. Though caught in a breeze
it rises like bubbles, twisting
as they slide along the shapes
of the folding air.

Did he show you how frail filaments
carried the future, glittered
silver under his microscope?

Child in a meadow. It's not
that the picture lies – *the face
of nature bright with gladness* –
but the knowing that, even
as we watch, *ten thousand
sharp wedges* are driving
into the beloved face. For even
in banks of flowers he could read
the *incessant blows.*

For the airy down, drifting,
catching the light, is charged
to drive a deep root,
brute aside the smothering
grasses. And while he studies
the intricate brilliance of barnacles,
rampant bacilli are invading
the joy of his heart.

That roll of the dice.
And living the searing price,
still, he could rejoice.

Green Man in a Chapel

Apropos of Darwin's Orchid –
Angraecum sesquipedale

You ask why I'm gagged
with ash boughs, gagged
like a witch – you ask why
I grimace. It's what you've
made of me. Hear a stone tale.

I'm hung by a window, lapsing
into traceries that garland the light –
an effigy. Compelled
to witness, by bell and candle
your ritual incantations.

I never felt the need for spells.
Wherever I walked Spring
danced behind me. You've seen
how beauty will still a room?
My power was simple presence.

My passage set the thicket
singing, the new wheat
flowing like water. Mine
was the breath of moth wings
on pale, moon-staring flowers.

You think me an old romantic?
Consider the stalking dapple,
the soaring raptor's binocular stare.
Rock and wildwood were my
cradle for tooth and claw.

Now study this wasting image,
the dust that grinds and levels:
it beds my seed. Where cracks
in your pathways are greening,
hear my whisper:

                     It's Yggdrasil
springing
            from my mouth.

Sky Lines – Otterspool Promenade

For Eleanor and Hans

Soaring, dipping,
gold and scarlet –
a flame tied to a tether.
Then it tugs the eye
up and up
beyond the narrowing glare
into the cobalt zenith
so far. So
deep.

And the Mersey ebbing,
ruffled grey, a bit
baffled
by a warm west wind.

Such contrary forces.

White plumes
rise over Wirral –
breath of refineries.
Wirral, *Wirheal* –
place of bog myrtle –
a lost planet.

And above us – rippling,
streamers
like a comet – exuberance
made flesh. It hawk-
stoops. Climbs.

Bikes thrum
past. Folk
saunter through the sun.

Reclaimed from rubbish,
this promenade, this green.

And the boy with the kite
stands on his inheritance
intent on climbing
through the roof of the world.

For Charlotte
28th November, 2009

Born while an afternoon moon
  waited its moment,
while fog beyond us stretched
  under palest blue
like a new land distilled
  from roseate sunlight.
While three hawthorns, stark,
  thin-fingered, reached
in urgent, wooden gestures
  through the haze of their breath
and jackdaws broke from silence.
  While a white house
sat quietly in its meadow,
  fulfilling under the seeping
cold its modest purposes.

  And just at that moment
something proclaimed itself,
  electric, tactile,
a harmony fingering the spine,
  that even as we passed,
slid back into its elements –
  a house, the trees,
a gust of jackdaws, fog
  and a pale sky,
the swollen moon – but left
  a confirmation of arrival.

Walking

Monday 6th September, 2010

One…two… Lotte is learning
to walk. Three… four… she
wobbles. Claps. Her hands and arms
flail. Five… She flumps. Grins.
Topples into the air. Stands.

Where will you walk, child?
Can we keep a world for you?
Pay this joyous attention
to all that grows, needs nurturing?
And they try so hard for us.

Not only from the horizon's edge,
this dawn rose like breath
from the earth – that lemon light
in the hills. Trees were turbulent,
the sky serene, skerried in dove blue.

Then the day closed over us –
a drowning – but surely, secretly,
with our complicity? Things stretch
towards us like hands.
But difficult to bear – responsibilities.

Hawthorns are red-eyed,
hips glossed to bursting,
rose-madder ribs of willow herb
split, set loose an infinite
future. They grow on dereliction.

The air is thick with renewal.
It cartwheels over the stubble.
Swallows chatter on the wires,
flirt with a north west wind.
And fifteen hesitant steps….

The Open Road

For Emily

She stops to examine a snail.
'It's going home,' she says.
How do you know?
'It's squeezing back into its house.'
That gypsy life.
The open road.
'I've never touched a snail before.
Do slugs have bones?'

At times you catch a gleam
of where there is to get to.

Art Lesson

For Nick Wright

Red fox flowing
through a green field.
Stay, fox. Stay.

He stops. Looks over
his shoulder, trots
into a hedge. The field
is changed, charged,
the winter wheat greener.

Why does it take a fox
to clear the eye? To put
the day on tiptoe?

She saw. But remains
preoccupied, content
in her own revelation:
What did you do
at nursery today?

We climbed ladders
and painted fireworks
on the sky.